MECHANICS·
MERCANTILE
LIBRARY.

Arthur F. Mathews '06

# *The* *Missing Link*

by
SYDNEY BANKS

INTERNATIONAL HUMAN RELATIONS CONSULTANTS INC.

*i*

*The Missing Link*

© 1998 by Sidney Banks
First printed in 1998   10 9 8 7 6 5 4 3 2
Printed in Canada

Published by

INTERNATIONAL HUMAN RELATIONS CONSULTANTS INC.

Distributed by Lone Pine Publishing

| In the US: | In Canada: |
| --- | --- |
| 1901 Raymond Ave. SW, Suite C | 206, 10426 – 81 Ave. |
| Renton, WA  98055 | Edmonton, AB  T6E 1X5 |
| USA | Canada |
| 1-800-518-3541 | 1-800-661-9017 |

Canadian Cataloguing in Publication Data

Banks Sydney.
  The missing link

  ISBN 0-9681645-0-1 (Standard HC ed.)

  1. Spiritualism (Philosophy) I.Title.
B841.B36 1998         141         C98-910147-9

Senior Editor: Nancy Foulds
Production Manager: David Dodge
Layout & Production: Rob Weidemann
Book Design: Richard Mayer
Cover Design: Richard Mayer
Printing: Friesens Corporation, Altona, Manitoba

# $\mathcal{D}$edication

*In admiration of the*

*many people throughout*

*the world who encounter*

*suffering every day and*

*try to alleviate it.*

*The Missing Link*

# Contents

| | |
|---|---|
| Foreword | vii |
| Preface | xi |
| Introduction | xv |
| The Missing Link | 1 |
| The Theosopher | 11 |
| Three Principles | 19 |
| Mind | 29 |
| Consciousness | 37 |
| Thought | 45 |
| The Duality of Life | 65 |
| Seeking Enlightenment | 77 |
| Selecting a Teacher | 87 |
| Living in the Now | 97 |
| Feelings | 109 |
| Love & Forgiveness | 115 |
| Wisdom | 125 |

# *Foreword*

Throughout the history of psychiatry and psychology there has been an attempt to understand the workings of the human mind, both healthy and unhealthy.

The first century of the science of psychology has yielded hundreds of theories and disciplines. For the most part, these various schools of thought have produced inconsistent results and have often contradicted one another.

What has been missing is an understanding of the basic underlying, universal principles that will unify the field of psychology and give the healing results so badly needed in our troubled world.

In this simple book lies the profound missing link that will bring into sharper focus our attempts to help our fellow human beings. If we have the courage and humility to listen to the wisdom of these principles, they will direct us to a renaissance— not only for our field, but for humanity as a whole.

Over the years, as my own appreciation of these principles has deepened, I have come to see the power of Sydney Banks's message more clearly. My personal life has grown in ways I never dreamed possible. My professional work as a counselor, public speaker and consultant has far exceeded any dimension of success and effectiveness I anticipated. I have seen thousands of other professionals—and ordinary human beings—having the same kind of transformation as a result of the understanding presented in this book.

Take your time and savor each sentence over and over, and you too will reap the rewards.

*Joseph Bailey, M.A.L.P.*
*Author and Licensed Psychologist*

# *Preface*

The truth in this book speaks directly to the heart and soul of the reader. It opens the door to an inner life of stability and contentment which everyone intuitively knows, yet many have lost sight of in their daily pursuits. In the loving voice of an author who speaks from the certainty of enlightenment, this book offers solace to the world-weary, hope to the discouraged, direction to the lost and contentment to the discontented.

It speaks simply, yet with profound wisdom, of the inborn potential for the well-being, peace and happiness of all mankind which is accessible and near at hand. It illuminates the power of the human spirit in a way that transcends differences and evokes the best in all people. No one can read this book without being touched and inspired.

*Judith A. Sedgeman*

# *Introduction*

There are those in this world who believe miracles do not happen. I can assure such skeptics that they do.

With hope and faith as beacons, anything can happen.

*If these writings bring a second chance of life to just one human being, my work has not been in vain.*

*Sydney Banks*
*March 1998*

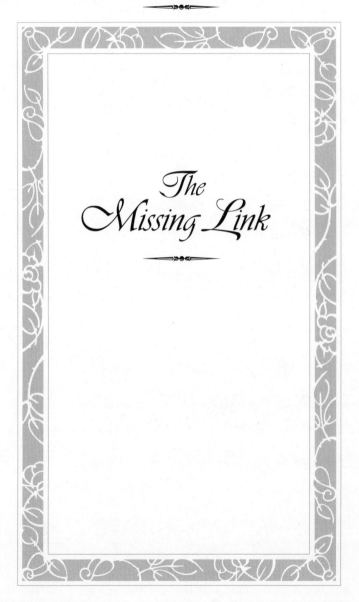

# The
# Missing Link

# *The Missing Link*

*O*ne of the greatest
misconceptions ever is the belief
that…

*"It takes years to find wisdom."*

Many experience time, few
experience wisdom.

The achievement of mental
stability and peace
of mind is *one* thought away from
everyone on earth… *if* you
can find that one *thought*.

Throughout time, human beings have experienced insights that spontaneously and completely changed their behavior and their lives, bringing them happiness they previously had thought impossible.

Finding wisdom has nothing to do with time.

Achieving mental stability is a matter of finding healthy *thoughts* from moment to moment. Such *thoughts* can be light years or a second away.

# The Missing Link

The spiritual energy of all things,
whether in form or formless, is
known by many names.

*Nature* is the physical form the
spiritual energy has taken.

Believe me, the subtle truth all
people seek will never be found
in the illusion of form called
nature.

Look deep inside your soul; this
is where you will find the answer.

*Your* thoughts and feelings are a
mirror of your soul.

Each living soul experiences life
as an individual. This is why all
humans live and see a separate
reality.

The divine truth that lies within
each living soul never changes. It
is eternal.

The divine passes from the
formless to form, and as human
beings we are both spectators and
participants in this spiritual
theater called life.

The great mystics of the world who tried to explain such knowledge had no choice but to speak in metaphors, knowing their words were only a representation of the spiritual wisdom that lies within the consciousness of *all* human beings.

*All human psyches are rooted in universal truth and no person's psyche is better than any other's. Only to the degree of the individual's psychological and spiritual understanding does it appear to vary.*

Words are merely a form. Listen not to words, but to *that which words attempt to convey.*

Remember… *it is not the clay that represents the sculpture, but the form the artist has molded it into.*

Just like the clay of the sculpture, *thought* is not reality. However, our personal realities are molded via our thoughts.

## The Missing Link

At the moment of birth, the
virgin mind discovers *creation*,
and the duality of life is born.
Henceforth you live in a world
governed by *thought*.

When clarity and purity of
thought are present, the answer
you seek will present itself, for
what you seek is with you and
has been with you always.

In the silence of our minds lies
creative incubation, bringing the
wisdom and the joy we all seek.

# The Missing Link

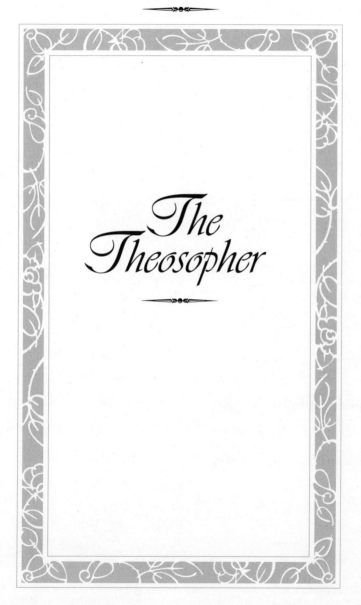

# The
# Theosopher

# The Missing Link

# *The Theosopher*

*P*hilosophers search for basic principles. They gain knowledge by reading books and studying other people's opinions and concepts, then mold them together with their own personal opinions of life.

A theosopher's understanding comes from a direct experience using his or her own *innate* knowledge, or if you wish, from what is sometimes known as *Original Thought*.

Philosophy examines the known
physical world. Theosophy hosts
both the world of form and the
formless.

To seek truth from the form alone
is only half the truth; it traps you
in a cosmic lie.

# The Missing Link

Everyone on earth is both a
philosopher and a theosopher.

One is a learned intellectual
process. The other is a realization
of knowledge from within the
depths of our own consciousness.

## The Missing Link

Such knowledge cannot be
bought or sold like a commodity
in the marketplace, nor is it found
in some far-off land.


It is hidden in the depths of
your soul.


This is why such knowledge can
only be found through an insight
from one's *own* inner wisdom.

Everyone in this world shares
the same innate source of
wisdom, but it is hidden by the
tangle of our own misguided
personal thoughts.

# The Missing Link

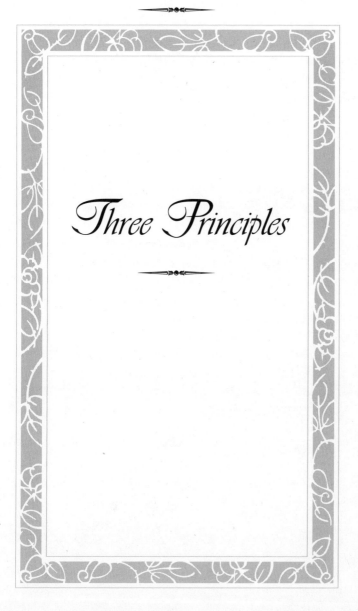

# Three Principles

# The Missing Link

# Three Principles

*M*ind, *Consciousness* and *Thought* are the three principles that enable us to acknowledge and respond to existence.

They are the basic building blocks, and it is through these three components that all psychological mysteries are unfolded.

They are what I call the psychological trinity.

*Mind, Consciousness* and *Thought* are spiritual gifts that enable us to see creation and guide us through life.

All three are universal constants that can never change and never be separated.

All philosophies are born via these three gifts and are a direct result of the correct or incorrect usage of these same principles.

All psychological functions are born from these three principles.

## The Missing Link

All human behavior and
social structures on earth are
formed via *Mind, Consciousness*
and *Thought*.

In chemistry two or more
elements create compounds. It is
the same with the psychological
elements... *Mind, Consciousness*
and *Thought*. These three
elements create psychological
compounds that are our own
personal psychological realities.

Healthy compounds – feelings,
such as compassion, humility,
love, joy, happiness and
contentment – are all rooted
in *positive* thoughts.


Hate, jealousy, insecurity, phobias
and feelings of depression are all
compounds of *negative* thoughts.

All feelings derive and become alive, whether negative or positive, from the power of *Thought*.

No matter what you *think* about, it has to be a compound. Even if you disagree with what I say, it's your *thought*.

All three elements – *Mind, Consciousness* and *Thought* – are the lifeline to our very existence. It is through these three elements that we have the power to realize the very existence of life.

Mental functioning cannot possibly exist without the three psychological elements. They are the building blocks of all mental behavior.

There are no more, nor any less, than these three. They create all human experience.

# The Missing Link

---

*Mind, Consciousness* and
*Thought* are the complete
Trinity of all psychological
functioning. Without one the
others are non-existent.


All living creatures, great or
small, interpret what they
think of life via these three
divine gifts.

# The Missing Link

*Mind*

# The Missing Link

# Mind

*Every human mind has direct access to its experience here on earth, and the human mind always has access to its own spiritual roots… from whence it came.*

The *Universal Mind,* or the *impersonal mind,* is constant and unchangeable.

The *personal mind* is in a perpetual state of change.

All humans have the inner ability to synchronize their *personal mind* with their *impersonal mind* to bring harmony into their lives.

Some believe the brain and the mind are the same. But there has to be a power behind the brain to make it function.

The brain and the mind are two entirely different things.

The brain is *biological*.
The mind is *spiritual*.

The brain acts like a computer: whatever you put into it is all you get out. This is *logic*.

## The Missing Link

An important thing to realize
is that *Universal Mind* and
*personal mind* are *not* two minds
thinking differently, but two
ways of using the same mind.

The world in the form of nature is a *reflection* of the human mind, which creates an *illusionary gap* between the spiritual and the physical.

This gap, in turn, creates the *duality of life*. Trapped in this duality, our minds become full of disillusionment and lostness.

As the human mind ascends in divine consciousness, the gap between subject and object begins to vanish and the oneness of life emerges.

# The Missing Link

There is one *Universal Mind*,
common to all, and wherever you
are, it is with you, always.


There is no end or limitation,
nor are there boundaries, to the
human mind.

# The Missing Link

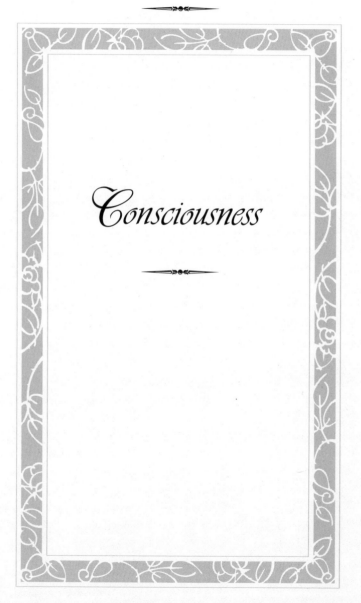

*Consciousness*

# The Missing Link

# Consciousness

All living creatures were given the power of *Mind*, *Consciousness* and *Thought*, which enables them to observe divine creation, or form.

Consciousness is the gift of awareness.

Consciousness allows the recognition of form, form being the expression of *Thought*.

Somewhere in the innermost
recesses of our consciousness lie
the answers to the questions all
mankind seeks.

As our consciousness descends,
we lose our feelings of love and
understanding, and experience
a world of emptiness,
bewilderment and despair.

As our consciousness ascends, we
regain purity of *Thought* and, in
turn, regain our feelings of love
and understanding.

Mental health lies within the consciousness of all human beings, but it is shrouded and held prisoner by our own erroneous thoughts.

This is why we must look past our contaminated thoughts to find the purity and wisdom that lies inside our own consciousness.

When the wise tell us to look *within*, they are directing us beyond intellectual analysis of personal thought, to a higher order of knowledge called *wisdom*.

Wisdom is an innate intelligence
everyone possesses deep
within their souls, before the
contamination of the outer world
of creation.

Find the spiritual wisdom that
will guide you through life from
within.

This is where you will find the
feelings of love, understanding
and contentment.

# The Missing Link

That the deaf man cannot hear
the sound of the crashing ocean
waves, or the blind man cannot
see the beauty of an autumn sky,
does not mean the sea and the
sky do not exist.

So, like the blind man, close
your eyes.

Like the deaf man, block your
ears; go inside and realize…that
which you seek has been there,
within you, all along.

This is when the blind will see
and the deaf will hear.

# The Missing Link

Thought

# The Missing Link

# *Thought*

*Thought* is a divine tool, nothing more, nothing less, only a tool. A wise person, like a good tradesman, uses this tool to the best of his or her ability.

The power of *Thought* is not self-created.

*Thought* is a divine gift, which serves you immediately after you are born.

*Thought* is the creative agent we use to direct us through life.

*Thought* is the master key that opens the world of reality to all living creatures.

*Thought* is the missing link that gives us the power to recognize the illusionary separation between the spiritual world and the world of form.

## The Missing Link

Thought on its own is a
completely neutral gift.

*Thought is not reality; yet it is
through Thought that our realities
are created.*

It is what we as humans put into
our *thoughts*, that dictates what
we think of life.

Among the greatest gifts given to us are the powers of free thought and free will, which give us the stamp of individuality, enabling us to see life as we wish.

These same gifts can also be the greatest weaknesses of humanity. We often lack the strength to change our minds, so we get stuck in the negative thoughts and behaviors of the past.

The purer your thoughts are, the more love and understanding will be in your heart.

# The Missing Link

Positive thoughts create a healthy
mind and a stable life.

Optimism is a spiritual quality
and a guiding light that will lead
you to your happiness.

Pessimism, on the other hand, is a
disease of the human thought
system that leads the thinker into
the darkness of despair.

Negative thoughts create
negative feelings, which in turn
create negative behaviors and are
the seeds of human suffering.

*"As you sow, so shall ye reap."*

*The Missing Link*

When our minds are in unity
with that which is good, then our
*thoughts* no longer hold us
prisoner to that which is evil.

When you start to see the power
of *Thought* and its relationship to
your way of observing life, you
will better understand yourself
and the world in which you live.

To find that which you seek,
discard all thought that there is
a separation between the *spiritual*
and the *physical* world.

The wise medicine men in the Native North American culture spoke of the world as *one* spirit, referring to the creator of all things as the *"Great Spirit."*

This was their way of explaining the oneness of life.

*Thought* is a divine tool that is the link between you and your divine inheritance, and is at the core of all psychological functioning.

## *The Missing Link*

You can't even be aware of
creation without the presence
of *Thought*.

*Thought* is the missing link
between mental sickness and
mental health. *Thought* is also the
missing link between happiness
and sadness.

Your *personal mind* activates
your thoughts and makes them
good or bad.

You have no control over what
others think, but you do have the
power to control what you think.

*Our thoughts are the camera, our eyes are the lens. Put them together and the picture we see is* reality.

In the silence beyond all things lies the divine knowledge that will help guide you through life.

Look *within your own consciousness*, for here lies the answer to all of humanity's problems.

## The Missing Link

———�ný⟨ý⟩ŷ———

Your thoughts are like the artist's brush. They create a *personal* picture of the reality you live in.

*Thought*, like the rudder of a ship, steers us to the safety of open waters or to the doom of rocky shores.

The wise man says,
"I think, therefore, I am."

The fool says,
"I don't *think* so."

*The Missing Link*

People often speculate how many components there are to thought.

There are no components to thought. *Thought* is a divine power. It is an element that can never be broken down into smaller segments.

It is we human beings that use *Thought* to produce such things as our feelings, moods and our overall perceptions of life.

*Thought* can be used in an *infinite* number of ways.

## The Missing Link

The more we dwell on the positive side of life, the more *hope* becomes a beacon, attracting positivity into our lives and guiding us to a steadfast and more contented way of life.

Many people make the mistake of believing that their moods create their thoughts; in reality, it is their thoughts that produce their moods.

The *personal mind* is the creator of all activity. The *personal mind* is the creator of all misery, all expectations, all ideas and all false deities.

# The Missing Link

Hope and faith go together. With hope and faith in your heart, you will find the perfect path you seek.

When the desires of your mind
trouble your spirit, your life
becomes turmoil. My advice is to
learn to free yourself from too
many desires.

Life on earth is short, so beware
of striving for fame and fortune.
Many who find them never live
to enjoy them.

Many people would succeed in life if their ambitions weren't so above their abilities.

Many who strive for the moon begin their journey by tripping over their own feet.

Everything on earth comes from one divine source. Our personal thoughts determine what we think of the form it has taken in our lives.

*Thought* is related to our five senses.

Our senses have no ability to discriminate. They are controlled and informed by our personal power of *Thought*. Without *Thought*, our five senses would be of no value.

*The Missing Link*

Our five senses and our egos
are but particles of the whole, just
as the illusion of time and space
are only particles of the whole.

The answer people seek lies not
in their separate beliefs, but in the
realization that *Thought* is the
common denominator in all
psychological and spiritual
understanding.

# The Missing Link

# The
# Duality of Life

# The Missing Link

# *The Duality of Life*

*N*ature is a cosmic illusion suspended within the boundaries of time, space and matter.

When one awakens from this illusionary dream state, it is known as the *Great Awakening*.

When people search for truth, they often look in two directions – at the form and at the formless – creating the idea of a duality in life.

# The Missing Link

*The life force beyond all
things has no form, yet it gives
form to all things.*

# The Missing Link

In the illusory world of thought,
many believe the *inner self* is God
and the *outer self* is the body. But I
can assure you, the inner self and
the outer self are the same thing.

Your eyes must see in the
singular if you want to find truth.

When you understand this, you
will see through the illusionary
duality of life.

*All life is divine energy,*
*whether in form or formless.*


When this energy takes form,
we call it nature.


Both the form and the
formless together create the
whole, the *oneness* of life, that
which we call God.

## The Missing Link

Nothing can possibly be greater
or separate from the whole. Only
the ego suffers such delusions.

Our *personal mind*, or what
is sometimes referred to as the
ego, galvanized with our
consciousness, equals our reality
in its entirety.

Our ego, combined with our five
senses, often creates distorting
lenses that stop us from evolving
to our true spiritual nature.

# The Missing Link

At times we are captivated by our own ego and become prisoners of our contaminated thoughts.

Ego creates self-importance and is strictly related to the personal self and the personal intellect.

The ego creates duality and separates us from the great divine oneness and the wisdom we seek.

## The Missing Link

Do not try to understand the
words of the wise from an
intellectual perspective.

Listen for a positive *feeling*.

Positive feelings will bring you
the answer you seek. Delving
into the workings of your ego
won't.

# The Missing Link

Do not ponder on the subject of ego. If you do, your labor will be in vain.

Focus on the *missing link* between our psychological nature and our spiritual nature.

The truth you seek does not come from books or the spoken word, but from within the soul of humanity.

Nothing on earth can be more
paradoxical than truth, for truth
represents both the form and the
formless.

Without one, the other is only
half the puzzle.

Without one, the other is of
little value and is a cosmic lie.

As we start to regain the
true relationship between our
*personal intelligence* and the
*spiritual wisdom* that lies within,
we develop a higher degree of
intelligence and common sense.
This, in turn, clears up our
misguided lives.

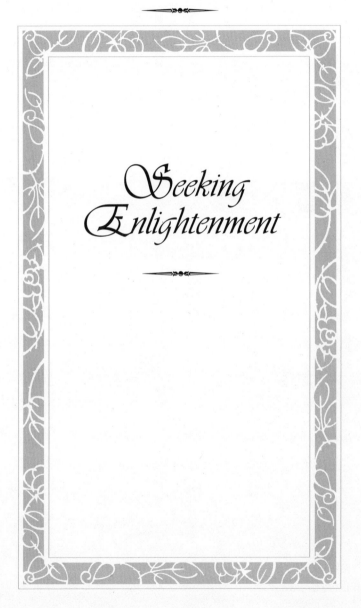

# Seeking
# Enlightenment

# The Missing Link

# Seeking Enlightenment

We all seek enlightenment whether we are aware of this fact or not, and my friend, I tell you this...

*Purer thoughts* are the rungs of the ladder that lead to success.

The Universal center of all things, we call God.

The individual center, we call a soul.

In the depth of our souls, we discover our divine inheritance.

*It is not the power of the word or the determination of our might, but the deep and silent workings of our minds which bring the* inner self *and the* outer self *together, into harmony.*

This is why many try to silence their minds through meditative contemplation. They seek a purer state of *Thought*.

# The Missing Link

My words may seem too
simple, but I say again, the truth
*is* simple.

Look for common sense; plain,
old-fashioned common sense.

When seeking wisdom, one is
very apt to find that in simplicity
lies complexity. Those who don't
realize the profound nature of
such simplicity are very apt to
expound on their findings,
losing the essence.

Look for psychological *logic…*
*the logic of the psyche.*

Before the formation of physical
reality and the contamination of
*personal* thought, *soul* and
*consciousness* were the same
divine intelligence.

# The Missing Link

Cut off from innate wisdom, a lost thinker experiences isolation, fear and confusion.

This is why there are so many horrible atrocities throughout the world. Newspapers are full of wars, killings, children starving.

Ignorance of our own inner wisdom is the cause of sin. There would be no sin without such ignorance.

The malfunction of our own personal thought system instigates the breakdown of personal relationships and leads to the crumbling of societies, causing unnecessary suffering and sadness.

The misled *thoughts* of humanity, alienated from their inner wisdom, cause all violence, cruelty and savagery in this world.

Since the beginning, the state of any society is a direct result of its conditioned way of thinking.

## The Missing Link

As you think, so you shall hear.

*The sage hears fools*
*and wise alike.*

*The fool hears only fools.*

# The Missing Link

# Selecting a Teacher

# The Missing Link

---

# Selecting a Teacher

There are so many teachers in the world and so many theories about life. When selecting a teacher, ask yourself…

Is my teacher a well-balanced person?

Is she or he happy?

Does my teacher reflect and demonstrate the quality of life I desire?

If the answer to any of these questions is no, move on in your journey. Otherwise you may become one of the blind, led by the blind.

*The Missing Link*

I have great admiration for the clergy and therapists of this world. They are both helpers of humanity; only their approach and words differ.

The preacher attempts to purify our souls.

The therapist attempts to purify our consciousness.

Originally, psychology examined the connection between *mind* and *soul*, until that theory was abandoned.

When psychologists stopped investigating the connection between *mind* and *soul*, they lost two of the most important clues to what they sought.

They focused instead on behavior, leading us away from our true psychological nature, ultimately encouraging us as passive victims of life.

From behaviorism a multitude of techniques arose. But I can assure you, techniques are to therapists as rituals are to the church. They lead you away from the very truth you seek.

Please realize, I am not condemning current teachings. I am simply saying that many don't realize the importance of finding one's *own* inner wisdom.

There is an enormous difference between finding your *own* inner wisdom and adopting someone else's beliefs.

# The Missing Link

If you take on someone else's belief to replace a belief of your own, you may experience a temporary placebo effect, but you have not found a lasting answer. However, if you replace an old belief with a realization from *your* own inner wisdom, the effect and results are superior and permanent.

It is one thing to *listen* to the words of the wise and quite another to be a *follower*.

Any good teacher will tell you never to be a follower. A wise teacher will draw out your innate knowledge.

## The Missing Link

Followers fail. They readily adopt another's beliefs and cease to think for themselves.

*Never* follow the words of others blindly, or you will only take on another person's reality. You will only hinder your progress by seeking fool's gold.

*Use your own common sense.*

Beware of cults and organizations that want to strip you of your right to think freely.

If you become a *follower*, you lose your independence and become a slave to someone else's ideas and beliefs; you give up your *free will* and *freedom of thought*, two extremely valuable assets in life.

# The Missing Link

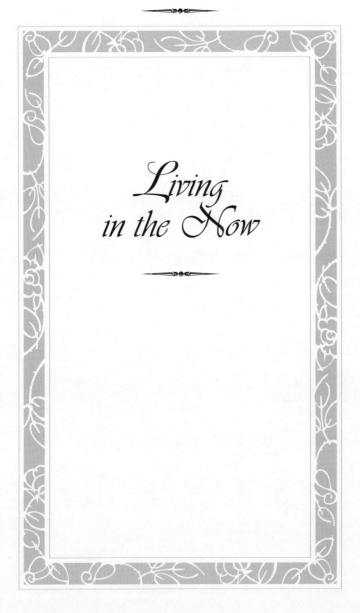

# Living in the Now

# The Missing Link

# Living in the Now

Through the centuries, the wise have told us to live in the *now*. This is why I say to you…

The past is a ghost that cannot be held in the palm of your hand.

The future cannot be grasped, no matter how desirable or enticing it may appear.

Nor can the present be held, no matter how beautiful or exciting.

Begin the process of nourishing the soul by living in the *now.*

Forget the past and the future, and *just be,* and you will surely be rewarded by living in the *now.*

When Eastern mystics describe the *now,* they are not talking about today as a specific day of the month and year. Their meaning goes deeper. When such people refer to the *now,* they mean the *personal mind* is free from the contaminants of yesterday's memories and fears.

This in turn frees the mind to see
with clarity things as they *are*, not
through distorted memories and
apprehensions.

Living in the *now* requires a
clear mind.

In clearing our minds, we may
have to give up something to
receive something.

If you wanted to replace a glass
of stale wine with fresh wine,
first you must pour out the old
wine. It is the same with clearing
our minds of unwanted, stale
thoughts.

*We must rid ourselves of yesterday's negative thoughts to receive today's new and positive feelings.*

I do not ask anyone to ignore their past experiences. This would be denial, and denial is *not* a healthy state.

Instead, seek a clearer understanding of the past; realize that the negative feelings and emotions from past traumatic experiences are *no longer* true. They are merely memories, a collection of old, stale thoughts.

# The Missing Link

As surely as rust slowly destroys the strongest steel, hate and negative thoughts erode the soul of humanity.

Negative thoughts are like scratches on a window: they stop you from seeing life with clarity. When the negative thoughts cease, the scratches disappear and the window becomes crystal clear. Then the beauty and positive aspects of life can be seen.

The past is dead. Forget what is old and dead, and start life anew.

Discard the restless, haunting
ghosts of yesterday and set
yourself free to live the beauty
of today.

Change the pattern of
your thoughts from negative
to positive; automatically the
condition of your life will change
for the better.

# The Missing Link

Just as the gardener rids a
garden of unwanted weeds, we
must rid our minds of
pernicious thoughts, which
like weeds crowd out the
beauty from our minds.

I call the process of casting
away negative thoughts a
*spiritual mind treatment*.

Our *thoughts* are our guide;
a good guide navigates
through the maze of life by
following the pathway of *love*
and *understanding*.

## The Missing Link

If your thoughts wander onto a negative and rocky path, don't take them too seriously.

Refrain from analyzing, because, I guarantee you, you will analyze yourself forever, never reaching an end, and fail bitterly to find peace of mind.

What happened in the past may have influenced our present-day personal or social problems, but please believe me, there is no answer to these problems in the past. Only in the now can the answer be found.

## The Missing Link

The intensity and importance of
such events dissipates as we see
that the past is *no longer a reality*,
but a *memory* carried through
time via our *own* thoughts.

Deal not with conditions of the
past, but look to the laws of cause
and effect. See the effect and
consequences *thought* has on
our everyday lives.

Seek simplicity and logic…
psycho-*logic*.

When your mind is full of
*negative thoughts*, you
automatically see and live
in a negative reality.

By the same rule, a mind centered on positive thoughts automatically lives in a far more pleasant reality.

Let your negative thoughts go. They are nothing more than *passing thoughts*. You are then on your way to finding the *peace of mind* you seek, having healthier feelings for yourself and for others.

This is simple logic.

# Feelings

# The Missing Link

# Feelings

Our *feelings* are the
barometer of our *thoughts*.

When the mind is filled
with positive thoughts, cause and
effect rule, resulting in a positive
*feeling*.

When the mind is filled
with negative thoughts, again
cause and effect rule, creating a
negative *feeling*.

Our *feelings* are evidence of our mental well-being. Find positive and loving *feelings*, for they will guide you through life far better than resentment and grudges.

Positive thoughts and feelings will assist you to discover the mental health and wisdom that lie within you.

When you learn to forgive those who have wronged you in the past, you clear your mind and bring harmony into your life, allowing you to see what *is*, instead of what *isn't*.

## The Missing Link

What isn't... *is life seen through distorted memories.*

What is... *is life seen as it truly is now, clear of all falsehoods.*

The tormented mind, which entertains love and forgiveness as guests, will surely attain new heights.

# The Missing Link

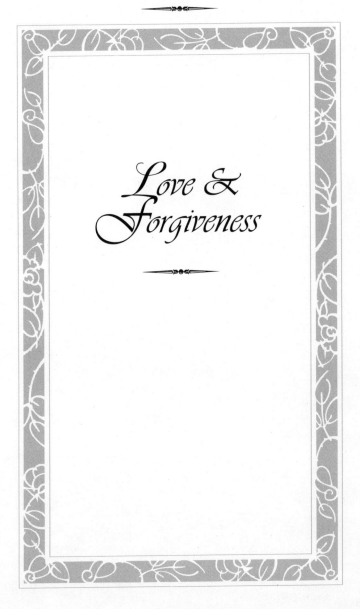

# Love &
# Forgiveness

# The Missing Link

# *Love & Forgiveness*

*Love* and *understanding* harmonize the mind of humanity to its true inner nature.

*What you give in life is what you receive.*

To give love is to receive love.

A mind full of love and good feelings can never go wrong.

*Love* and *forgiveness* go hand-in-hand. Without them, life is encumbered by ill feelings and unhappiness.

## The Missing Link

Judging your own faults or
the faults of others leads to
unhappiness. A mind that dwells
in non-judgment is a contented
mind.

A heart full of love is void of
all judgment and is filled with
divine spirit.

*My love is like a red, red rose;*
*Its fragrance fills the air;*
*It guides me to a place of light,*
*Instead of dark despair.*

## The Missing Link

Forgiveness is divine, and has wonderful effects on our lives.

Forgiveness is a powerful remedy to clear thoughts of negative memories. It frees us from the emotional prisons of our past, providing opportunities to start life anew.

Forgiveness brings forth peace of mind. Without forgiveness, the road through life is paved with doubt and misery.

An unforgiving mind burdens
one with negative thoughts,
holding onto yesterday's hurts. It
contaminates and prevents the
thinker from living a happy
life *now*.

It is forgiveness that allows you
to see today as a new experience.

God has already forgiven you
for yesterday's mistakes, so why
don't you forgive yourself?

To dwell on past trials and
tribulations is to *deny* the
moment.

If you live in the past, you can never find happiness. *You are trying to live in a reality that no longer exists.*

It is a misconception to think that if you forgive someone who has harmed you, you are somehow condoning their behavior, making yourself vulnerable so that you will allow them to repeat their hurtful action.

This is not so. There is a vast difference between forgiving a *person* and forgiving an *act*.

For example, say you were at the zoo and you approached a tiger's cage. If you were silly enough to put your hand through the bars and the tiger, being a tiger, ripped your hand open, you would probably have cursed the tiger. Later on, though, as you thought about it, you'd realize it really wasn't the tiger's fault. You would forgive the tiger. Yet you undoubtedly would have learned not to stick your hand into the cage again.

## The Missing Link

Forgiveness releases *you* from mental anguish and pain, and all the horrible negative feelings an *unforgiving mind* experiences.

When you learn to *forgive*, you see with clarity the ignorance and the innocence of those who trespass against you.

You realize that hanging onto old grudges is like a miser in deep water clutching at a bag of fool's gold, unaware that the fool's gold is just heavy, useless rocks weighing him down.

There is no way to guarantee a
trouble-free life.

Life is like any other contact
sport. You may encounter
hardships of one sort or another.

Wise people find happiness not
in the absence of such hardships,
but in their ability to understand
them when they occur.

*Wisdom*

# The Missing Link

# Wisdom

*Spiritual Wisdom lies within the consciousness of all living creatures*. It is formless. The second it is revealed to a human soul, it has taken on a form that can only represent its true nature.

In the old Hawaiian religion, the Kahunas or wise priests said the wisdom they were trying to convey was a secret that could not be told.

# The Missing Link

They were not intentionally
withholding the secret, but
literally could not convey it by
words alone, words only being
symbolic of their true meaning.

The answer sought is *beyond
the word*.

No one can give away wisdom.
A teacher can only lead you to it
via words, hoping you will have
the courage to look *within yourself*
and find it inside your *own*
consciousness…

*Beyond the word.*

## The Missing Link

The wisdom humanity seeks lies *within the consciousness* of all human beings, trapped and held prisoner by their own personal minds.

*Wisdom* is not found in the world of form, nor in remote corners of the globe. Wisdom lies *within our own consciousness.*

Only *you* have the golden key to your soul and the wisdom that lies within.

Those who refuse good advice
cannot be helped. Good advice is
seldom welcomed in the mansion
of a fool. Anyone who tries to
force learning on such a person is
indeed a fool as well.

To find wisdom, elevate your
consciousness. Seek a *grateful
feeling* for what you already have
in life.

# The Missing Link

Gratitude and satisfaction have wonderful effects on our souls. They open our minds, clearing the way for wisdom and contentment to enter.

Once you become grateful, the prison bars of your mind will fall away. Peace of mind and contentment will be yours.

The ego and our intellect are functions of our personal minds, whereas wisdom is a function of the spirit. One is mortal, the other immortal.

Intellectual observation is ego, *after form*.

Wisdom is found before the formation of form.

Ego is only what you *think* you are and what you think of life, nothing more, nothing less.

Our intellect and our inner wisdom should work together to create harmony in our lives. However, if the intellect lacks wisdom, chaos reigns. This is the state of the world today.

# The Missing Link

Those who have found a balance
between their intelligence and
their innate wisdom are the lucky
ones.

As human beings we must
look closely at the relationship
between our spiritual nature and
our psychological nature.

Here we will find the answers
we seek to change the deplorable
state of the world.

The consciousness of humankind must be elevated. Only then, when the spiritual and physical realities are united, will we find the power and intelligence to guide us through life.

Wisdom cleans the channels of your mind and brings sanity into your life.

*You must find it for yourself.*

Pure soul and pure consciousness
can only temporarily be separated
by the erroneous thoughts of
humanity because *soul* and
*consciousness* are one and the
same.

Wisdom is divine nourishment
for the soul; it is a God-given
intelligence before the
contamination of form or
personal thought.

With wisdom people see *beyond* the filters and biases of race and culture, to realize the beauty in everyone.

Such understanding enables people to stop fearing and distrusting those who are different, to see the commonality of human beings regardless of cultural differences.

Wisdom applied to society would do more than anything else to halt the ethnic clashes and wars the world suffers from today.

## The Missing Link

Wisdom is impersonal.

Wisdom is immortal and unchangeable.

Wisdom is the path to all spiritual understanding.

Wisdom is also the path to all psychological understanding.

## The Missing Link

———❧———

Our psychological nature
and our spiritual nature are
entwined, and the more they are
harmonized, the more contented
we will be.

Wisdom brings *common sense to
those who find it*.

# The Missing Link

The solutions to outwardly complex problems created by misguided thoughts will not arise from complicated analytical theory, but will emerge as an insight, wrapped in a blanket of simplicity.

Trying to deal with marital problems, for example, using a variety of methods and techniques may meet with little or no success. However, when a lost couple finds *wisdom* and *understanding* within their *own* consciousness, their marital problems will start to dissipate.

Seek without seeking, for what you hope to attain is already within you.

# The Missing Link

*That which you seek has no form.*

If you attempt to put a shape on the formless, you will never find it.

Attempt to describe the formless with words, and the word turns the formless into form, creating an illusion and leading you further away from that which you seek.

## The Missing Link

There are many ways to find the
inner wisdom that will lead you
to a healthier state of mind.

*You must exercise your*
*freedom of choice to decide on*
*your own individual path.*

No matter which path you take,
the wisdom you seek will always
be found within the depths of
your *own* consciousness.

*Bless those who*
*have sinned against you,*
*For they have lost their way.*
*Reach out your hand*
*and help them*
*To live a happy day.*

The End